Peterson Field Guides®
For Young Naturalists

Bizarre Birds

Jonathan P. Latimer
Karen Stray Nolting

Illustrations by Roger Tory Peterson

Foreword by Virginia Marie Peterson

Houghton Mifflin Company
Boston 1999

D0068153

FOREWORD

My husband, Roger Tory Peterson, traced his interest in nature back to an encounter he had with an exhausted flicker when he was only 11 years old. When he found what he thought was a dead bird in a bundle of brown feathers, he touched it and the bird suddenly exploded into life, showing its golden feathers. Roger said it was "like resurrection." That experience was "the crucial moment" that started Roger on a lifelong journey with nature. He combined his passion for nature with his talent as an artist to create a series of field guides and paintings that changed the way people experience the natural world. Roger often spoke of an even larger goal, however. He believed that an understanding of the natural world would lead people — especially young people — to a recognition of "the interconnnectedness of things all over the world." The Peterson Field Guides for Young Naturalists are a continuation of Roger's interest in educating and inspiring young people to see that "life itself is important — not just our-selves, but all life."   **—Virginia Marie Peterson**

Copyright © 1999 by Houghton Mifflin Company
Foreword copyright © 1999 by Virginia Marie Peterson
All illustrations from *A Field Guide to the Birds* copyright © 1980 by Roger Tory Peterson and
A Field Guide to Western Birds copyright © 1990 by Roger Tory Peterson.

Special thanks to Dick Walton for his expert advice.

All rights reserved. For information about permission to reproduce selections from this book, write to Permissions, Houghton Mifflin Company, 215 Park Avenue South, New York, New York 10003.
PETERSON FIELD GUIDES is a registered trademark of Houghton Mifflin Company.

Library of Congress Cataloging-in-Publication Data
Latimer, Jonathan P.
Bizarre birds / Jonathan P. Latimer & Karen Stray Nolting ; illustrations by Roger Tory Peterson ; fore-word, Virginia Marie Peterson. p. cm. — (Peterson field guides for young naturalists) Includes index.
Summary: A field guide to odd birds such as roseate spoonbills, snail kites, anhimas, burrowing owls, and greater prairie chickens.
ISBN 0-395-95213-1 (cl). — ISBN 0-395-92279-8 (pbk.)
1. Birds—Juvenile literature. 2. Birds—Identification—Juvenile literature. [1. Birds.] I. Nolting, Karen Stray. II. Peterson, Roger Tory, 1908–1996, ill. III. Title. IV. Series.
QL676.2.L372 1999   598—dc21   98-35512 CIP AC

Photo Credits
American Flamingo: Isidor Jeklin; Roseate Spoonbill: Caulion Singletary; Pileated Woodpecker: Gary W. Carter; Red Crossbill: Warren Greene; Chimney Swift: Mike Hopiak; Black Skimmer: Lawrence Wales; Arctic Tern: Mary Tremaine; American Oystercatcher: Lawrence Wales; American Dipper: James Sanford; Snail Kite: L. Page Brown; American White Pelican: Allen Cruickshank; American Anhinga: Isidor Jeklin; Common Loon: John Gavin; Atlantic Puffin: Steve W. Kress; Roadrunner: R. D. Wilberforce; Burrowing Owl: L. Page Brown; Greater Prairie Chicken: Mary Tremaine; Cliff Swallow: Mary Tremaine; Whooping Crane: Rob Curtis/VIREO; California Condor: S. LaFrance/VIREO.

Book design by Lisa Diercks. Typeset in Mrs Eaves and Base 9 from Emigre
Manufactured in the United States of America
WOZ 10 9 8 7 6 5 4 3 2 1

CONTENTS

HOW TO WATCH BIZARRE BIRDS

An owl that lives underground?
A bird that walks underwater?
A chicken that dances to attract a mate?

These bizarre — or strange — birds are all real, and they are all found in North America.

Why do we think these birds are bizarre? A bird may be bizarre because it does something unique. It might hunt for food in an odd way or build a remarkable nest. It may be that a bird does something much better than other birds. It may fly faster or farther — or it may rarely fly at all. Or it may be that we think the bird simply looks strange.

The birds in this book are grouped by the characteristic that makes them seem bizarre. These characteristics are the first things you often notice when you see the bird, such as the peculiar bill of a Roseate Spoonbill or the daring flight of a Black Skimmer. Other qualities have been understood only after long study, such as the migration route of the Arctic Tern or the way flocks of White Pelicans hunt. Though you may know of other birds that seem stranger than those included in this book, these bizarre birds have been selected because they are all found in North America, which makes it more likely that you may be able to see them in the wild.

The illustrations of these birds are by the man who revolutionized bird identification, Roger Tory Peterson. He invented a simple system of drawings and pointers (now known as the "Peterson System") that call attention to the unique marks on each kind of bird. This book introduces the Peterson System to beginners and young birders.

Migration

In spring many birds migrate north to their nesting sites. In fall they move south to warmer areas where there is more food. For example, some terns migrate thousands of miles each year. This means that you may see bizarre birds as they pass through your area during these seasons.

Where Can You See a Bizarre Bird?

Many of the birds in this book can be found throughout North America, but some, such as the Snail Kite, live only in one place. Information about where each bird can be seen is found under the heading Habitat in the bird's description. If you happen to be near one of those places, be sure to look for that bizarre bird.

Recognizing Birds

Figuring out what kind of bird you've seen is like solving a mystery. You gather clues and eventually you can find the answer. With some bizarre birds you may need only one or two clues because they are so unusual. But for others you may need more clues. Solving the mystery can be a challenge, but it is also a lot of fun. Try not to get frustrated. You'll get better with practice. Here are some questions you can ask when trying to identify an unknown bird.

How Big Is the Bird? Size is a quick clue to identifying a bird. Is it larger than a sparrow? Is it smaller than a pigeon? The size of the bird will help you rule out some choices and concentrate on others.

What Is the Bird's Shape? The shape of a bird can also help you identify it, even when you can't see its color. Is the bird slender or plump? Does it have a long neck or long legs? What shape is its bill or tail?

What Color Is the Bird? Color may be one of the first things you will notice when you see a bird. But color alone is not always enough to identify it. While there are only a few birds that are pink or red, there are many that are brown or black or white.

Does It Have Any Field Marks? Many birds have marks such as spots or stripes on their feathers or colored bills or legs. These are called field marks. Field marks can be found on a bird's head, wings, body, or tail. A puffin, for example, has a brightly colored bill, and a Pileated Woodpecker has a red crest on its head. As you get used to looking at birds, noticing field marks will become a very quick way to identify them or to tell similar birds apart.

What Is the Bird Doing? As you watch birds you may notice that they behave in certain ways. Some of these behaviors are good clues to the bird's identity. This is especially true with bizarre birds. If you see a large bird with long legs running across the desert, it is probably a Roadrunner. If you hear a bird drumming on a hollow branch, it is probably a woodpecker. As you become more familiar with certain birds, you will be able to identify them by their behavior alone.

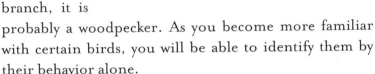

What Does It Sound Like? Some birds have calls or songs that you will recognize immediately. The *coo, coo, coo* of a Mourning Dove or the *cheep, cheep* of a House Sparrow are familiar sounds. The yodeling, mournful wail of the Common Loon — that sounds like *ha-oo-o* — is more bizarre, but once you've heard it you will never forget it.

A Couple of Tips

Many people keep a list of all the birds they have ever seen. This is called a Life List. You can begin yours with the list on page 48. It includes all the birds described in this book.

One more thing: keep your eyes on the bird for as long as you can. Watch it until you think you can describe it in some detail. Answer as many of the questions above as you can. Then check this book to identify the bird. Looking back and forth between a bird and your book might make you lose sight of the bird. They do fly away!

FLAMINGO

. . . has a unique way of eating

These rose pink wading birds have been copied in plastic so often that they have become a kind of joke, which is too bad because flamingos are graceful and beautiful birds.

A flamingo's bill is unlike any other bird's. It contains rows of bony plates that act like filters. A flamingo finds food by dipping its bill into the muddy bottom of saltwater bays. It sucks up the ooze and uses its tongue to force the mud out through these bony filters, leaving a rich meal of tiny crustaceans in its mouth. A flamingo feeds with its head upside down. Unlike the jaws of other birds, the flamingo's upper jaw moves up and down instead of its lower jaw.

Did You Know?

- A flamingo gets its pink color from the tiny crustaceans it eats. In zoos its color will fade to white unless it is given similar food. Roseate Spoonbills are the only other birds in North America that eat the same food, and they are also pink.
- Baby flamingos have a straight bill. During the first month after hatching, their bill grows downward into the shape of an adult's.
- Although there are flocks of wild flamingos in Florida, most of them have probably escaped from captivity. Wild flamingos are rare in North America, except on Caribbean islands. The flamingo's official name is American Flamingo.

FLAMINGO

Long neck held straight out

Black on wings visible

Legs straight

Males and females look alike.

Rose pink color

Very long neck

Long thin legs

Downward-curved bill with black on end

The neck of the Flamingo droops downward when it is feeding.

Habitat Flamingos are found on tropical seacoasts around shallow saltwater bays and lagoons.

Voice Flamingos make a honking noise that is similar to a goose's. It sounds like *ar-honk.*

Food Flamingos eat mainly microscopic animals found in the mud at the bottom of shallow ocean bays. They also eat tiny fish.

ROSEATE SPOONBILL

Looks aren't everything!

Spoonbills are very beautiful — except for that strange bill! They are graceful wading birds with rosy pink wings and a white back and neck. But it is their long spoon-shaped bill that gives them their name.

The Spoonbill's bill may look funny, but it is very useful for feeding. Roseate Spoonbills wade through shallow water, sweeping their bills back and forth through the mud on the bottom. The end of their bill has many nerves and is very sensitive. Spoonbills keep their bills partly open as they search through the ooze. When their bill senses a small fish or shrimp, it snaps shut. The Spoonbill then tosses its head back and swallows its prey.

Did You Know?

• Newly hatched Spoonbills do not have a spoon-shaped bill. This develops over the first few weeks of their lives.
• In the 19th century, Roseate Spoonbills became endangered because they were hunted for their feathers, which were used in hats and clothing. After World War I, fashions changed and Spoonbill feathers were no longer in demand. Laws were also passed to protect the Spoonbills, and their numbers have gradually recovered.
• Like flamingos, Roseate Spoonbills get their pink color from the food they eat.

ROSEATE SPOONBILL

Long flat
spoon-shaped
bill

White back
and neck

Red patch
on shoulder

Very pale
pink feathers

(Young)

Bright pink
wings and
chest

(Adult)

Orange
tail

Habitat Roseate Spoonbills are found in both fresh-water and saltwater marshes, lagoons, mud flats, and mangrove thickets in Florida and along the Gulf Coast.

Voice Although they are usually silent, Spoonbills make a low grunting croak when nesting.

Food Spoonbills catch small fish, shrimp, crayfish, crabs, beetles, and mollusks in muddy water.

PILEATED WOODPECKER

All that hammering!

Like all woodpeckers, a Pileated Woodpecker gets much of its food by pounding on tree bark with its bill. It

also carves holes in tree trunks with its bill to make a space for its nest. All that pounding would give most of us a big headache — but not woodpeckers. They have some remarkable characteristics that let them pound as much as they need to.

A woodpecker's head has strong muscles, and its skull is very thick. This helps absorb the shock of the pounding. A woodpecker's bill is shaped like a chisel and is very sharp. It hacks through wood like an ax. Woodpeckers have very long tongues that they use to pick up insects from trees.

Did You Know?

- The Pileated Woodpecker is the second-largest woodpecker in North America. The Ivory-billed Woodpecker is larger, but it may be extinct. None have been seen since the 1960s.
- If you see a large oval or oblong hole dug in the side of a tree, it may mean a Pileated Woodpecker is in the area.
- Pileated Woodpeckers are not common in most areas, but their numbers seem to be increasing.

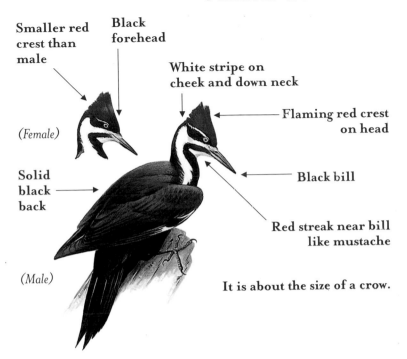

Smaller red crest than male

Black forehead

White stripe on cheek and down neck

Flaming red crest on head

(Female)

Solid black back

Black bill

Red streak near bill like mustache

(Male)

It is about the size of a crow.

Habitat Pileated Woodpeckers are found in forests, especially where there are large trees and many stumps. Pairs may stay in the same area year after year.

Voice The call of the Pileated Woodpecker is a loud, irregular *kik-kik-kikkik — kik-kik*. It also has a ringing call that may rise and fall in pitch.

Food Pileated Woodpeckers feed mainly on carpenter ants. They dig into the carpenter ants' nest by chiseling a hole in the side of a tree, then use their long tongues to catch the ants. Pileated Woodpeckers also eat other kinds of ants, termites, beetles, nuts, fruits, and berries. They sometimes strip bark off trees to get at larvae hidden beneath.

CROSSBILLS

A strange bill that makes a useful tool

Crossbills look a lot like the House Finches you probably see everyday, but they have one major difference. The tips of their bills overlap, forming an X-shape. This looks like it would make it hard for crossbills to eat, but it is perfect for prying seeds out of pine or spruce cones.

A crossbill doesn't grab the seed with its bill. It uses its bill to pry open the cone while it holds it with one foot. Then the crossbill removes the seed with its tongue. A crossbill also uses its bill and its feet to climb around trees like a parrot does.

Crossbills often twitter while they feed, but the sound you are most likely to hear is the noise of cones breaking.

Did You Know?

• Red Crossbills and White-winged Crossbills have similar habits and are sometimes seen together. White-winged Crossbills are a little smaller than Red Crossbills.

• The bill of a young crossbill is straight until after it has left the nest. Then it can cross either to the right or the left.

• Crossbills appear to be either right- or left-handed in opening cones — depending on which way their bill crosses.

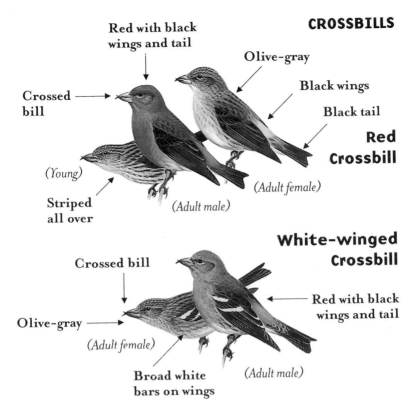

Red with black wings and tail

Olive-gray

Crossed bill

Black wings

Black tail

Red Crossbill

(Young)

Striped all over

(Adult female)

(Adult male)

White-winged Crossbill

Crossed bill

Olive-gray

Red with black wings and tail

(Adult female)

Broad white bars on wings

(Adult male)

Habitat Crossbills wander in small flocks, looking for food. They are found in forests or groves where there are trees with cones, such as pine, spruce, fir, or hemlock.

Voice The call of the Red Crossbill is a hard *jip-jip* or *jip-jip-jip*. Its song has finchlike trills and chips that sounds like *jip-jip-jip-jeeaa-jeeaa*. The call of the White-winged Crossbill sounds like *chif-chif*. Its song is a series of loud trills.

Food Crossbills eat mainly the seeds of cone-bearing trees. Red Crossbills eat mostly pine nuts and White-winged Crossbills eat mostly spruce seeds, which are smaller. Both also eat seeds and buds of other trees, some kinds of berries, and some insects.

CHIMNEY SWIFT

Speedy fliers that nest in odd places

Long ago Chimney Swifts built their nests in hollow trees, but today they use chimneys or airshafts or any dark, sheltered place in a building. They have even been known to nest inside wells.

The Chimney Swift's nest is made out of twigs that are glued to a flat surface in the shape of a shallow half-cup. Swifts attach each twig to the nest with their sticky saliva. As the saliva dries, it forms a cementlike surface that holds the nest together. Often dozens of Chimney Swifts nest together in one place.

During the day, Chimney Swifts spend all their time flying. They are active fliers and have been timed at speeds of around 20 miles per hour.

Did You Know?
• At night when they sleep, Chimney Swifts clutch the side of a chimney with their feet. They often crowd together so that their tails overlap like roof shingles.
• Chimney Swifts drink by dipping their bills into water while skimming over a pond or river.
• It has long been known that Chimney Swifts migrate, but where they go has only recently been discovered. A few birds banded in the United States have been found in the Amazon Valley of Peru.

Wings held in curve
when gliding

Dark gray all over

Males and females
look alike.

Tail barely visible

The Chimney Swift is sometimes described
as looking like a cigar with wings.

Habitat Chimney Swifts are seen most often flying
over cities and towns during the day. At night they roost
in chimneys and airshafts.

Voice The call of a Chimney Swift is a series of loud,
rapid ticking or twittering notes.

Food Chimney Swifts catch their food in the air. They
eat mostly flying insects, including beetles, flies, flying
ants and termites, and even spiders gliding in the air.

BLACK SKIMMER

. . . just skimming the water

Black Skimmers have the right name. When they hunt they skim just above the water's surface. The long lower part of their bill slices through the water like a knife. When their bill strikes a small fish, it snaps shut, catching the fish. But even with a fish in its mouth, a Black Skimmer doesn't stop flying. It lifts its bill out of the water, swallows the fish, and keeps on gliding.

Black Skimmers are steady fliers, moving slowly back and forth over smooth water near shore. When flying in flocks, the wings of the Black Skimmers beat in the same rhythm. When a flock turns, it seems to flash black and white as the birds show their black backs and white undersides.

Did You Know?
• Black Skimmers all face the same direction when they are resting on the sand together.
• The lower part of the Black Skimmer's bill grows at twice the rate of the upper part. This keeps it from being worn away by the friction caused by regularly dragging it through water.

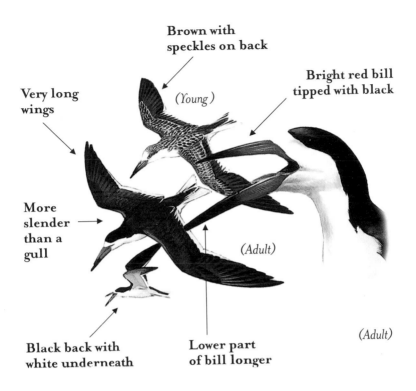

Brown with speckles on back

(Young)

Bright red bill tipped with black

Very long wings

More slender than a gull

(Adult)

Black back with white underneath

Lower part of bill longer

(Adult)

Habitat You are most likely to see Black Skimmers on ocean bays and inlets that are protected from rough surf. They also hunt on freshwater lakes and ponds. Skimmers nest on sandy islands, sandbars, and beaches.

Voice When they are alarmed, Black Skimmers make a barking call that sounds like *kak, kak, kak* or *kaup, kaup*.

Food Black Skimmers eat mostly small fish and minnows. They will also eat small crustaceans that float near the surface of the water.

ARCTIC TERN

Champion of long-distance migration

Even though this seabird is only about the size of a crow, it is a world-class traveler. Arctic Terns nest in the north far above the Arctic Circle. Each fall they fly south past the equator and spend winter hunting fish in the cold waters off Antarctica. In spring they return north again to nest. This is a round trip of more than 22,000 miles and most of it is over open ocean!

Like other terns, Arctic Terns hunt for food by diving into the ocean. They sometimes hover above the rough surface of the ocean until they see a fish. Then they dive straight down, plunging into the water to catch their prey with their bill.

Did You Know?
- Arctic Terns spend more time in daylight each year than any other animal. They are near the North Pole in summer when it has its longest days and near the South Pole during winter when it has its longest days.
- Arctic Terns defend their nesting sites so fiercely that even human intruders must carefully protect themselves.

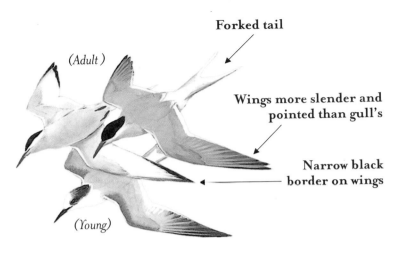

Forked tail

(Adult)

Wings more slender and pointed than gull's

Narrow black border on wings

(Young)

White forehead

Black bill

(Adult in winter)

Black cap

(Adult in summer)

Orange bill

White cheeks

Habitat Arctic Terns spend much of their time over the open ocean, but they can sometimes be seen near rocky coasts and islands, particularly in the Far North.

Voice The call of the Arctic Tern is a high, rasping *kee-yah*. They also make a call that sounds like *keer-keer*.

Food Most of the food eaten by Arctic Terns is fish caught near the surface of the ocean. They also eat small crustaceans, shrimps, insects, worms, and even berries.

OYSTERCATCHERS

. . . learn to open shellfish

Opening a clam or an oyster is difficult. It takes a young oystercatcher months to learn how. They learn by watching their parents. But once they know how, it takes them less than 30 seconds to open a shellfish. Some oystercatchers open shellfish by hammering and others by stabbing.

A hammerer pounds rapidly with its bill on a shell until it breaks a hole in it. It works its bill inside the shell and cuts the muscles that keep it closed. Then it opens the shell and cleans it out.

A stabber sneaks across the rocks looking for shell-fish with slightly open shells. Before the shell can close, it stabs its bill inside and cuts the muscles. Then it pries the meat out.

Did You Know?

• American Oystercatchers live on the East Coast, and Black Oystercatchers live on the West Coast.
• If an intruder approaches a family of oystercatchers, the adults will fly away. The young will flatten themselves on the ground and sometimes hide their heads under the grass.

OYSTERCATCHERS

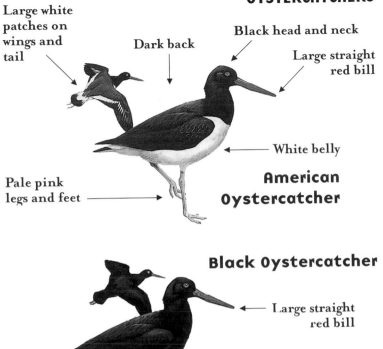

Large white patches on wings and tail

Dark back

Black head and neck

Large straight red bill

White belly

American Oystercatcher

Pale pink legs and feet

Black Oystercatcher

Large straight red bill

Black all over

Pale pink legs and feet

Habitat Oystercatchers are found only along the coasts, especially on rocky beaches or tidal flats where there are beds of oysters or clams. They nest on sand dunes or on islands in saltwater marshes.

Voice The call of an oystercatcher is a sharp *wheep!* or *kleep!* American Oystercatchers also make a loud *pic, pic, pic.*

Food Oystercatchers eat mostly mussels, clams, and, of course, oysters. They also eat other shellfish, such as limpets and barnacles, and marine worms, crabs, and sea urchins.

AMERICAN DIPPER

A bird that walks underwater?

Many birds can swim and dive underwater, but American Dippers actually walk on the bottom of rushing mountain streams. They swim to the bottom, then run along, poking under stones searching for insect larvae to eat.

American Dippers have some amazing adaptations for hunting underwater. Their bodies are covered with a thick layer of down and soft feathers. This keeps their skin warm and dry when they dive into the icy water. Dippers also have a flap that covers their nostrils when they are underwater and special membranes that protect their eyes. Their wings and tail are short and stubby, but they are useful in both water and air. American Dippers sometimes "fly" underwater through rushing streams, pushing with their wings.

Did You Know?
- American Dippers can dive as deep as 20 feet below the surface of a stream.
- When they fly in the air, dippers follow the path of the stream, rather than traveling over dry land.
- American Dippers don't migrate. When streams in the mountains freeze during winter, they move to lower altitudes where the water is not frozen.

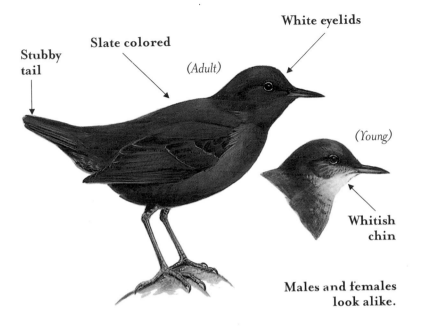

Stubby tail

Slate colored

(Adult)

White eyelids

(Young)

Whitish chin

Males and females look alike.

An American Dipper is shaped like a wren but is about the size of a robin.

Habitat Dippers are found around fast-flowing streams and creeks in the mountains of the West, especially at high altitudes.

Voice The song of the American Dipper is high and bubbling. It is loud enough to be heard over the sound of rushing streams. The dipper's sharp call sounds like *zeet.*

Food The primary food of American Dippers is insect larvae that live in the water. These include mayflies, beetles, mosquitoes, and many others. They also eat snails, worms, fish eggs, and very small fish.

SNAIL KITE

Special prey for a picky eater

The curved bill of the Snail Kite is used to pull snails out of their shells. When a Snail Kite sees a snail, it flies down and grabs it with one foot. The Snail Kite carries it back to its perch and works the snail out of its shell.

Snail Kites hunt only one kind of snail, the apple snail. This has led to their becoming endangered. Apple snails depend on fresh water to survive. In years of drought, they become scarce. Without other sources of food, Snail Kites become scarce as well. As the marshes of the Florida Everglades have been drained for farming or development, Snail Kites have been squeezed into a smaller area. There are perhaps as few as 700 left.

Did You Know?
- Snail Kites have a floppy flight when they are hunting. They don't need to fly fast—the snails aren't likely to run away.
- Snail Kites can pull a snail out of its shell without breaking the shell.
- Snail Kites are also known as Everglades Kites.

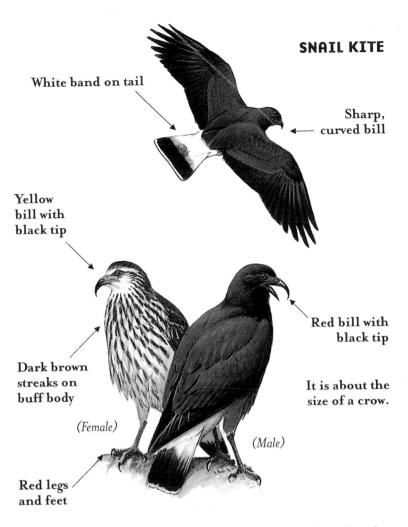

SNAIL KITE

White band on tail

Sharp, curved bill

Yellow bill with black tip

Red bill with black tip

Dark brown streaks on buff body

It is about the size of a crow.

(Female)

(Male)

Red legs and feet

Habitat In North America Snail Kites are found only in freshwater marshes and along canals and the shallow shores of lakes in central and southern Florida. They are more widespread in Central and South America.

Voice The call of the Snail Kite is a cackling *kor-ee-ee-a, kor-ee-ee-a.*

Food Snail Kites hunt only one kind of large snail. They are commonly known as apple snails. Scientists identify them as *Pomacea.*

27

WHITE PELICAN

Catching fish by working together

A White Pelican swims on the surface of water to catch fish. This is unlike most other birds that hunt in water, including the Brown Pelican, a close relative. A White Pelican dips its large bill into the water and scoops up water and fish in its pouch. It holds its bill downward to let the water drain out before it swallows the fish.

Sometimes White Pelicans fish in an even more unusual way. A flock will form a long line and swim across the water, beating their wings to drive fish ahead of them. They slowly form a circle, surrounding the fish. Then they move together in a tight bunch and dip their bills into the water to catch the fish.

> ### Did You Know?
> • Flocks of White Pelicans often form a single-file line as they fly. Individuals fly with their heads drawn back and their bills resting on their chests.
> • With a wingspan of almost 9 feet, the White Pelican is one of the largest birds in North America.
> • The White Pelican is officially known as the American White Pelican.

WHITE PELICAN

Black on wings →

Dark feathers on back of head

Males and females look alike.

Yellow-orange bill

Large white bird

(Young)

Grayish bill

(Adult)

During nesting season adults have a prominent ridge on their bills.

Habitat During nesting season White Pelicans are found on islands in inland lakes and rivers. During winter they are found in marshes and shallow bays along both coasts.

Voice Although usually silent, White Pelicans make low groans when they are together in their colony. Young pelicans sometimes squeal.

Food White Pelicans eat mostly fish, and sometimes crayfish or salamanders.

ANHINGA

How many names can a bird have?

This unusual long-necked diving bird is sometimes called a Darter because of the way it hunts fish. The Anhinga chases fish deep underwater and spears them with a darting thrust of its sharp bill.

Anhingas have also been called Snakebirds because they swim with only their neck and head above the water's surface. From a distance they can easily be mistaken for a water snake.

Anhingas are also known as Water Turkeys. They often stand in the sunlight with their wings and tails spread. Their spread tails reminded people of a turkey.

The name Anhinga was finally chosen to avoid confusion. It is the name given to this bird by Native Americans living near the Amazon River. Its official name is American Anhinga.

An Anhinga looks like a cormorant, but its neck is more snakelike and its bill is pointed.

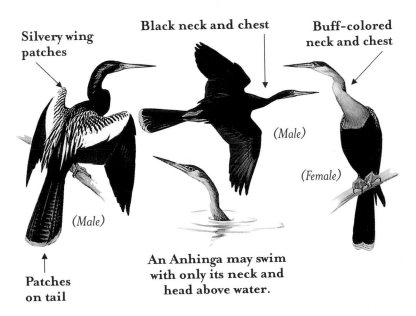

Silvery wing patches

Black neck and chest

Buff-colored neck and chest

(Male)

(Female)

(Male)

↑
Patches on tail

An Anhinga may swim with only its neck and head above water.

Habitat Marshes, swamps, and ponds in warm areas are home to the Anhinga. They can also be found on inlets and mangrove lagoons along the southern Atlantic and Gulf Coasts.

Voice Anhingas are silent most of the time, but they sometimes make rapid clicking sounds or hoarse croaks.

> **Did You Know?**
> • Anhingas fish in fresh water and avoid salt water.
> • Anhingas eat their prey at the water's surface. They often toss the fish into the air and swallow it headfirst.
> • Anhingas sometimes fly very high and soar overhead like hawks.

Food Anhingas hunt mostly fish, spearing them with their pointed bill. They also eat crayfish, shrimp, frogs, and insects.

COMMON LOON

Wild laughter on the water

If you are out in the woods on a dark summer night, the haunting cries of the Common Loon can send chills down your spine. The sound rises and falls and may remind you of crazy laughter.

Common Loons are actually shy birds, so you will probably hear one long before you see it. When you do see one, it will probably be swimming. They often paddle around the surface with their heads partially submerged, looking for food. A loon's legs are located far back on its body. This makes loons powerful swimmers, but it also makes them very clumsy on land. Because of this, loons spend most of their time on water, even sleeping there.

Males and females look alike.

Green head

Red eyes

Dark back

(Winter)

Thick, straight bill

Black and white collar

(Summer)

Black and white checkered back

Pale underneath

Habitat In summer Common Loons are found mostly on lakes in pine forests. They spend winter only on lakes that are large enough to stay free of ice or on the ocean.

Did You Know?

• Loons have been known to dive to depths of 200 feet and stay underwater for 2 to 3 minutes.

• Young Common Loons sometimes ride on a parent's back. They can dive and swim underwater when they are only two to three days old.

• Fossils show that ancestors of today's loons lived more than 65 million years ago.

• The loon's laughing call may be where the terms "crazy as a loon" and "loony" come from.

Voice The yodeling, mournful wail of the Common Loon sounds like *ha-oo-oo.* Loons call during both day and night in spring and summer. They are usually silent in winter. In flight they give a barking *kwuk.*

Food Common Loons eat many kinds of small fish, including minnows, perch, and sunfish.

PUFFINS

Their large colorful bills can hold lots of fish!

A puffin may remind you of the penguins you see in the zoo. Both are black and white birds that stand upright on land. Both have round bodies and short legs that make them clumsy walkers. Both are graceful swimmers and experts at catching fish. But puffins can fly and penguins cannot. Also, puffins have large bills that look like a parrot's and penguins do not.

A puffin's bill is a great tool for catching small fish. The puffin grabs a fish with the sharp tip of its bill. Then it holds the fish crosswise in the back of its bill with its tongue while it swims after another fish. Its bill can hold as many as 30 fish at one time!

Did You Know?
• Puffins can dive more than 200 feet deep.
• Puffins nest in burrows dug by both parents, usually in large colonies near other burrows. A burrow can be 7 feet long.
• Puffins wave their brightly colored bills to signal to each other in crowded colonies, especially during nesting time.

PUFFINS

Males and females look alike.

Gray cheeks

(Adult in winter)

Yellow bill

Bill tipped with red

(Adults in summer)

White cheeks

Bright orange feet

Colorful bill shaped like a triangle

Atlantic Puffin

Large orange bill shaped like a triangle

White face

Tufted Puffin

Curved ivory-yellow tufts of feathers around ears

Dark chest

No ear tufts

Dark face

Males and females look alike.

(Adult in winter)

(Adult in summer)

Habitat Puffins hunt near seacoasts and far out at sea. Atlantic Puffins are found along the coast of Maine and eastern Canada. Tufted Puffins live along the Pacific Coast.

Voice Puffins are usually silent.

Food Puffins hunt mostly small fish, but they also eat squid, shrimp, and sea worms.

ROADRUNNER

A bird that would rather run than fly?

Unlike the one in the cartoon, real roadrunners do not spend their time racing coyotes — but they can run through a patch of cactus at over 15 miles an hour! These long-legged birds hunt by walking around until they see their prey. Then they dash forward and catch it with their bill. Roadrunners also fly short distances and even jump into the air to catch flying insects.

Roadrunners stay in an area all year. They also mate for life. Both parents build the nest and care for their young. In fact, the male spends more time sitting on the eggs than the female does, especially at night. When young roadrunners leave the nest, they may travel long distances before they set up their own nests.

ROADRUNNER

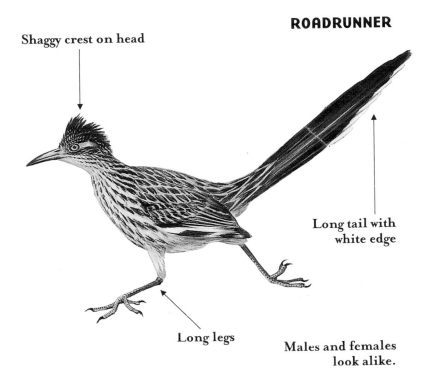

Shaggy crest on head

Long tail with white edge

Long legs

Males and females look alike.

Habitat Roadrunners are found in dry open country, especially deserts or areas with scattered brush.

Voice The call of a road-runner is 6 or 8 *coos* that sounds like a dove's call.

Food Roadrunners catch snakes and lizards, taran-tulas and scorpions, and mice, squirrels, and birds.

Did You Know?
- When it is surprised, a roadrunner will run away, which is where its name comes from. Its official name is Greater Roadrunner.
- Adult roadrunners pretend to be injured to lure intruders away from their nest.
- A roadrunner twitches its tail and raises the crest on its head when it is excited.

BURROWING OWL

A bird that lives underground?

Most birds live in trees, but Burrowing Owls make their home under the ground. They dig their own burrow or take over holes deserted by prairie dogs, ground squirrels, or other animals. Burrowing Owls use

their powerful feet to enlarge the other animal's burrow for their own use. They scrape away the soil and kick it into a mound outside the hole. They sometimes use this mound as a lookout for predators such as coyotes and foxes.

When threatened, Burrowing Owls do not take flight. Instead, they duck into their burrow. If the intruder tries to enter their burrow, the Burrowing Owl makes a noise like a rattlesnake to scare it away.

Did You Know?

- The Burrowing Owl's burrow can be as long as 10 feet.
- Stories have been told that Burrowing Owls live in the same hole with prairie dogs or even rattlesnakes. This is not true. Each animal lives in its own burrow.
- Cowboys nicknamed Burrowing Owls "howdy birds." This is because Burrowing Owls bob and bow when disturbed, making what looks like a friendly greeting.

Males and females look alike.

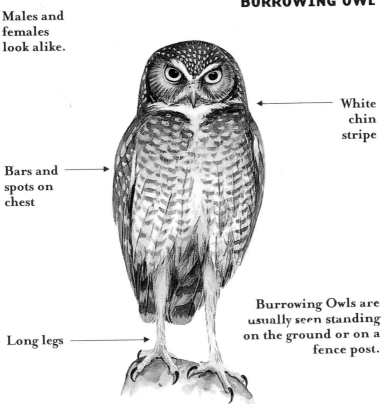

White chin stripe

Bars and spots on chest

Burrowing Owls are usually seen standing on the ground or on a fence post.

Long legs

Habitat Look for Burrowing Owls in open country, such as prairies, grassland, and farmland, where the grass is short or the soil is bare. They can also be seen around golf courses, airfields, and vacant lots.

Voice At night Burrowing Owls make a mellow *co-hoo* call that sounds like a Mourning Dove's *coo,* only higher. They also make a rapid chattering that sounds like *quick-quick-quick.*

Food Burrowing Owls usually hunt large insects, such as grasshoppers and crickets, and small rodents, such as mice, rats, and ground squirrels. They also eat lizards, toads, and snakes.

GREATER PRAIRIE CHICKEN

A spectacular courtship dance

During courtship male prairie chickens come together to dance. They gather on a hill or rise where they are sure to be seen by females. The males lower their heads, spread their tails, and hold their wings open at their sides. They inflate brightly colored air sacs in their necks and raise tufts of feathers over their heads. Then they strut about, calling and making an unusual boom-

ing sound. They stamp on the ground and sometimes leap into the air, challenging each other. A female prairie chicken selects her mate from the dancing males.

Today prairie chickens are found in only a few places in the Midwest. Much of the open grassland where they lived has been turned into farms and towns.

Did You Know?
• A male prairie chicken makes the booming sound by forcing air out of the sacs in his neck.
• The smaller, quieter Lesser Prairie Chicken is found farther west and in much smaller numbers than the Greater Prairie Chicken.

GREATER PRAIRIE CHICKEN

Males and females look alike.

Rounded dark tail

Black feathers straight up over head

Dark feathers on neck

Brown with dark brown bars

(Male during courtship dance)

Rounded dark tail

Orange sacs on neck

Habitat Greater Prairie Chickens are found on open prairies with tall grass in the Midwest.

Voice During courtship male prairie chickens make a "booming" call that sounds like *oo-loo-woo* — similar to the noise you make when you blow across the neck of a bottle.

Food Prairie chickens eat mostly seeds and leaves, although they sometimes eat insects such as grasshoppers and beetles. They also eat seeds from farmers' fields.

CLIFF SWALLOW

Nests that look like apartments?

Like most swallows, Cliff Swallows are remarkable fliers and excellent at hunting flying insects. But Cliff Swallows have one very unusual habit — they build their own apartment houses wherever they nest. A Cliff Swallow's nest is made out of mud and shaped like a bottle with a small opening on its side. These nests are built side by side, sometimes forming colonies that include thousands of nests.

Cliff Swallows build their nests under any kind of overhang, often under the eaves of a roof of a house or barn or even under a bridge or highway overpass. The overhang protects their mud nest from melting in the rain. One nest attracts other Cliff Swallows, and soon many nests appear side by side.

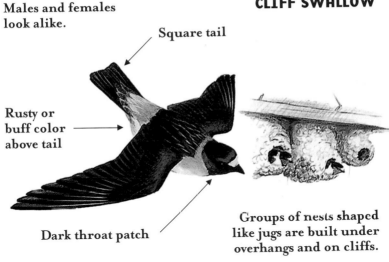

Males and females look alike.

CLIFF SWALLOW

Square tail

Rusty or buff color above tail

Dark throat patch

Groups of nests shaped like jugs are built under overhangs and on cliffs.

Habitat You may see Cliff Swallows near almost any kind of open land, especially near lakes. They live on farms or near cliffs or bluffs.

Voice The song of the Cliff Swallow is a harsh creaking sound. They also make noises that sound like *zayrp* or a low *chur*.

Food Cliff Swallows do most of their hunting while flying, catching insects such as beetles, wasps, bees, and flying ants. They also hunt grasshoppers, spiders, and moths and sometimes eat berries.

Did You Know?

• Cliff Swallows that are unsuccessful in finding food return to the colony. They watch successful hunters feed their chicks and then follow them to their hunting grounds.

• Cliff Swallows return to the same site year after year. The famous swallows that return to San Juan Capistrano Mission in southern California are Cliff Swallows. Their return has been celebrated on March 19 every year since 1776.

WHOOPING CRANE

On the way back from extinction

Standing more than 4 feet tall, Whooping Cranes are the tallest birds in North America. Their courtship "dance" is like a ballet. The partners bow to each other, toss grass into the air with their bills, and leap while flapping their wings.

The Whooping Crane is also one of the most endangered birds because the areas where they spend winter

have been turned into farms or homes for people. Their last wintering site, in Aransas, Texas, was protected by law, but by 1947 there were only 15 Whooping Cranes left in the wild. In 1954 their nesting area was discovered in the Far North and a recovery program was begun. Soon their numbers began to grow. Today there are more than 150.

Did You Know?

• The distance from the Whooping Cranes' nesting site in Canada to their wintering area in Texas is more than 2,400 miles. They migrate in pairs or small family groups.

• Whooping Cranes mate for life.

• Whooping Crane chicks leave the nest a few hours after hatching.

The tallest wild bird in North America, it stands over 4 feet tall.

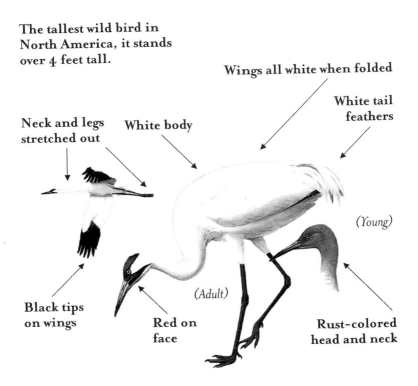

Wings all white when folded

White tail feathers

Neck and legs stretched out

White body

(Young)

Black tips on wings

(Adult)

Red on face

Rust-colored head and neck

Males and females look alike.

Habitat In winter Whooping Cranes are found on open prairie near pools and marshes. In spring and summer they nest in northern Canada.

Voice When flying Whooping Cranes make a shrill trumpeting cry that sounds like *ker-loo! ker-lee-loo!*

Food Whooping Cranes eat almost any kind of plant or small animal found near ponds or marshes. They eat seeds, roots, and berries and catch insects, snails, frogs, snakes, and small fish.

CALIFORNIA CONDOR

Moving toward survival

The California Condor is the largest bird in North America. It has a wingspan of more than 9 feet. A scavenger, it soars over the countryside on warm air currents, looking for dead animals.

In the 1800s, California Condors lived throughout the West. But by the early 1980s, hunting and the use of the pesticide DDT had reduced their number to fewer than 25. To save the California Condor, scientists captured all the wild condors. They planned to breed them in captivity for later release.

By 1987 all of the wild California Condors had been placed in zoos. In 1992, scientists began releasing young condors born in captivity back into the wild in California. Additional condors have been released near the Grand Canyon.

Did You Know?
- There are only about 100 California Condors left today.
- In the wild, California Condors spend much of the day sitting. When the air becomes warm enough to provide currents for them to ride, they begin looking for food.
- Female California Condors lay 1 egg every other year. It takes five to six months for a young condor to learn to fly and another six months before it is on its own.

A California Condor is about
twice the size of a Turkey Vulture.

Yellowish orange head ← *(Adult)*

Gray head *(Young)*

Large white patches under wings

When flying, a California Condor's wings are
held in a flatter V than a Turkey Vulture's.

Habitat The California Condors being released in the
wild are found in protected areas in the mountains
north of Los Angeles and near the Grand Canyon. All
others are in captivity.

Voice California Condors are silent.

Food In the wild, California Condors eat freshly killed
animals, especially large animals such as deer and cattle.
At one time they were known to feed on dead whales and
seals washed up on the seashore. There is no record of a
California Condor ever attacking a living animal.

47

Jones Library, Inc.
43 Amity Street
Amherst, MA 01002

WITHDRAWN